All About Chile

by Monica Brown

HOUGHTON MIFFLIN BOSTON

PHOTOGRAPHY CREDITS: **Cover** © Francesc Muntada/CORBIS **1** © Masterfile (Royalty-Free Division). **3** © Blaine Harrington III/CORBIS. **4** © Francesc Muntada/CORBIS. **5** Craig Lovell/Alamy. **6** Dave Watts/Alamy. **7** David W. Hamilton/ Getty Images. **8** © Kevin Fletcher/CORBIS. **9** John Warburton-Lee/DanitaDelimont.com/ drr.net. **10** Lee Foster/drr.net.

Printed in China

ISBN-13: 978-0-547-02950-4
ISBN-10: 0-547-02950-0

9 10 11 0940 15 14 13
4500443494

Chile is a country in South America.
In Chile there are mountains,
deserts, and forests.
There are lakes, rivers, and beaches.
There are even volcanoes!

Pretend you are going to Chile for a trip.
I wonder what you will visit first.
You could go to the Atacama Desert.
The ground is covered with sand, and it almost never rains there.

Then you could go to the mountains.
Chile has grand mountains
called the Andes.
The Andes stretch a long way down
one side of Chile.

On the other side of Chile
lies the Pacific Ocean.
So Chile sits between
the Andes mountains
and the Pacific Ocean.

Chile has many rain forests.
The forests are filled with
fluttering birds.
The world's smallest deer, the *pudu*,
live in the forests of Chile.

In Chile, many people live on farms.
They grow food such as apples
and peaches.
Other people live and work
in big cities such as Santiago.
Santiago is Chile's largest city.
It is the capital of the country.

Children who live in Chile
go to school, just like you do.
They study math and reading,
just like you do.
But their classes are usually
taught in Spanish.

People in Chile are very friendly.
Someone might ask you to come over for dinner!
If you accept, you might have meat and vegetables.
You can express your thanks by saying "Gracias!"

If people gave prizes to friendly countries, Chile might win. If people gave prizes to beautiful countries, Chile might win also. Maybe you will visit someday, for real—not pretend!

Responding

TARGET VOCABULARY Word Builder

Make a word web around the word prize. What things can be a prize? Copy this word web and add more words.

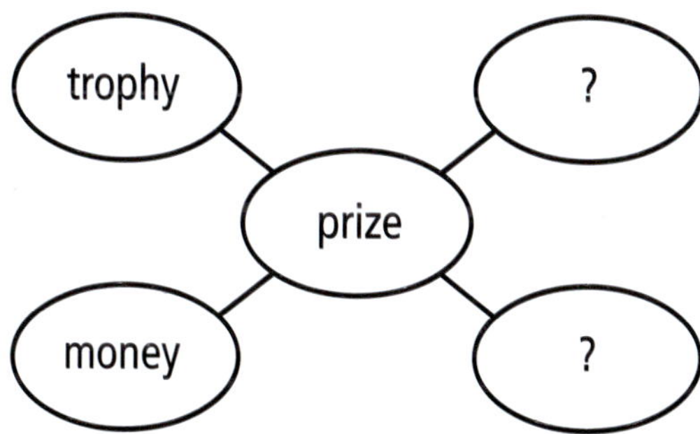

Write About It

Text to World Choose a prize from the Word Builder. Write a few sentences about the prize and what makes it special.

accept	pretend
express	prize
fluttering	taught
grand	wonder

TARGET STRATEGY **Analyze/Evaluate** Tell how you feel about the text, and why.

Word Teaser What do you do when you have a question?